AnNura Muhammad

Copyright © 2019 AnNura

ISBN:
9781702793100

DEDICATION

To the young black child reading this. You can do anything you put your mind to. Grow up and make the impossible, possible and create the world you want to live in. Be great.

I am almighty.

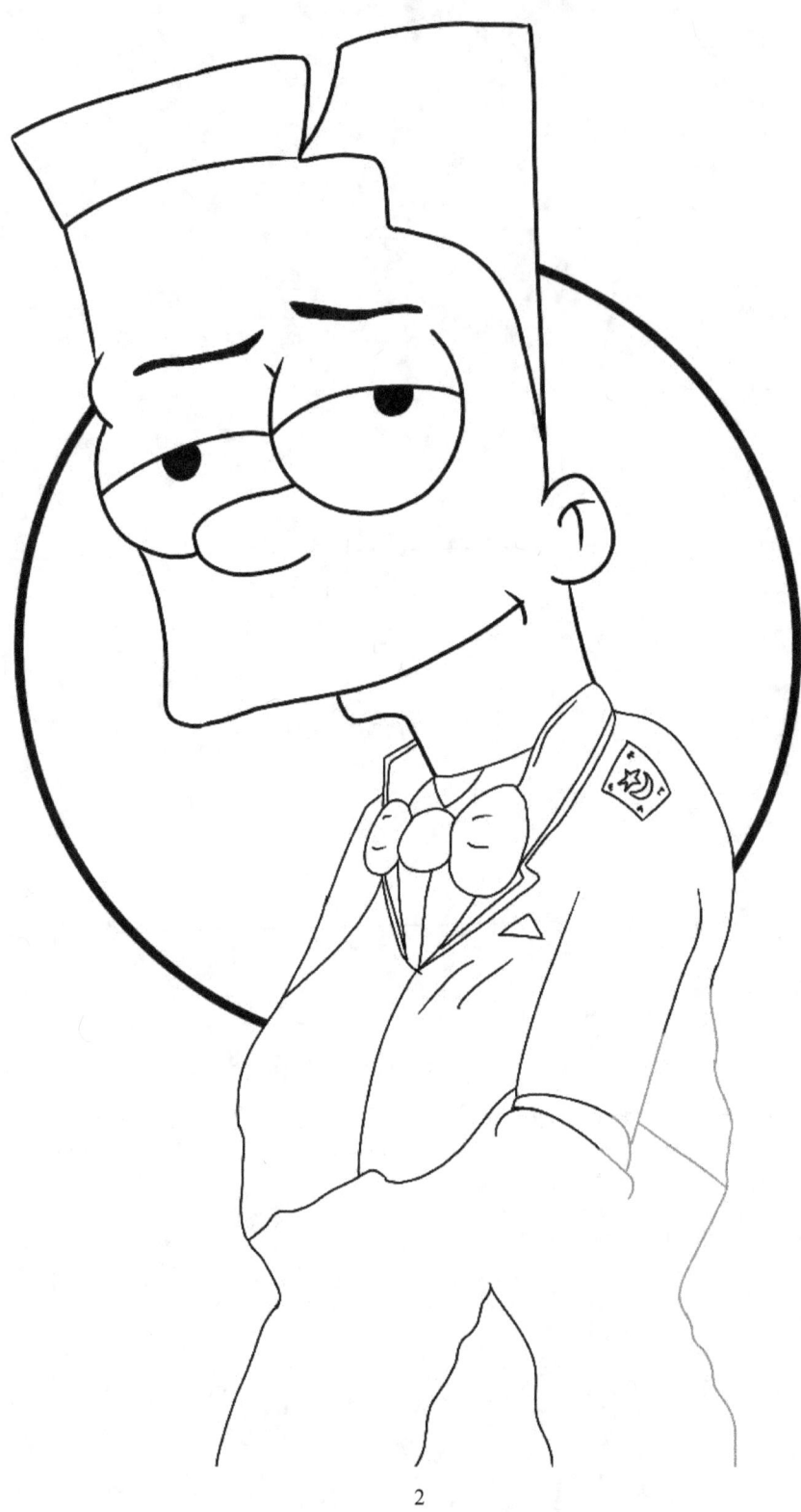

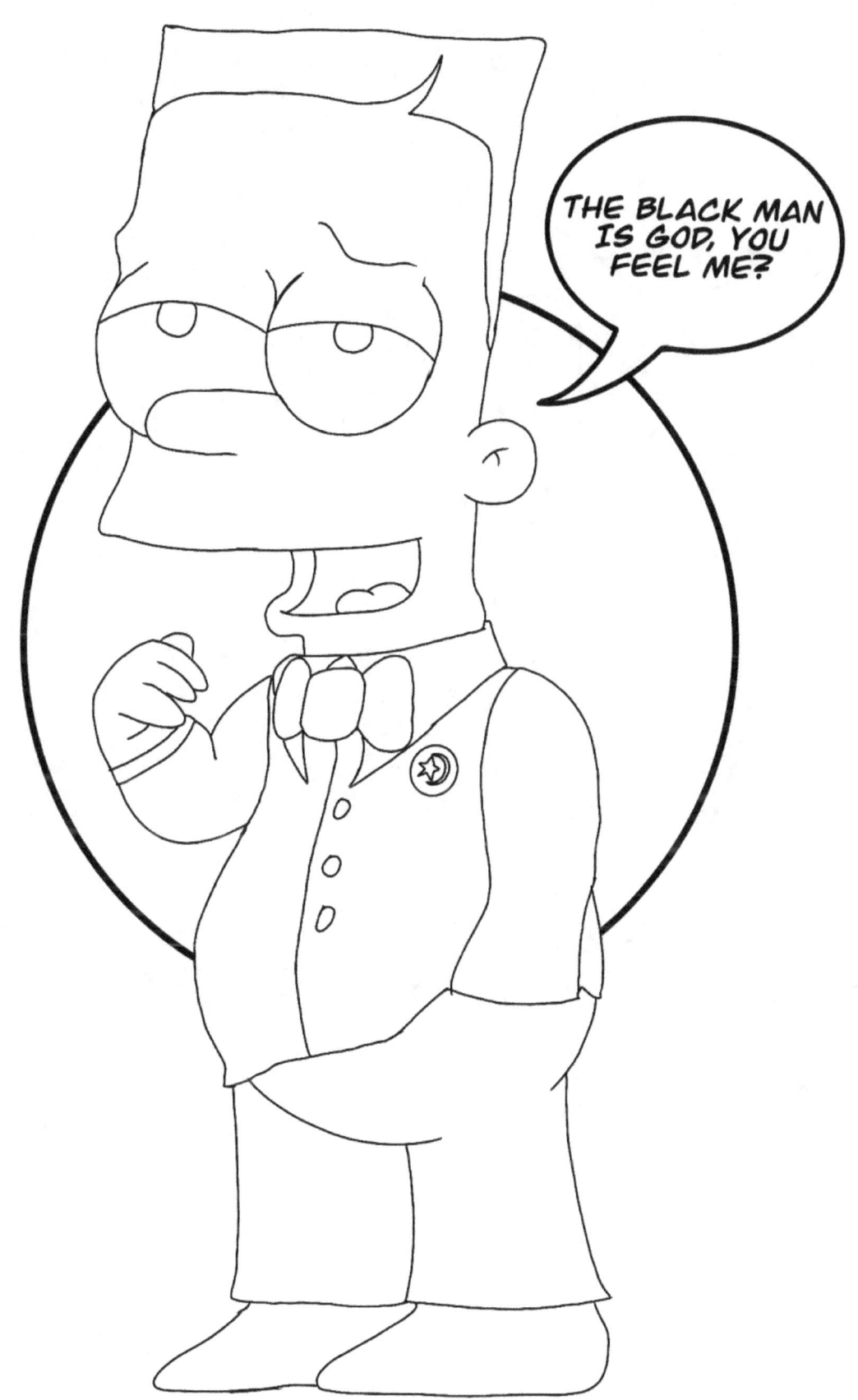

I am a princess.

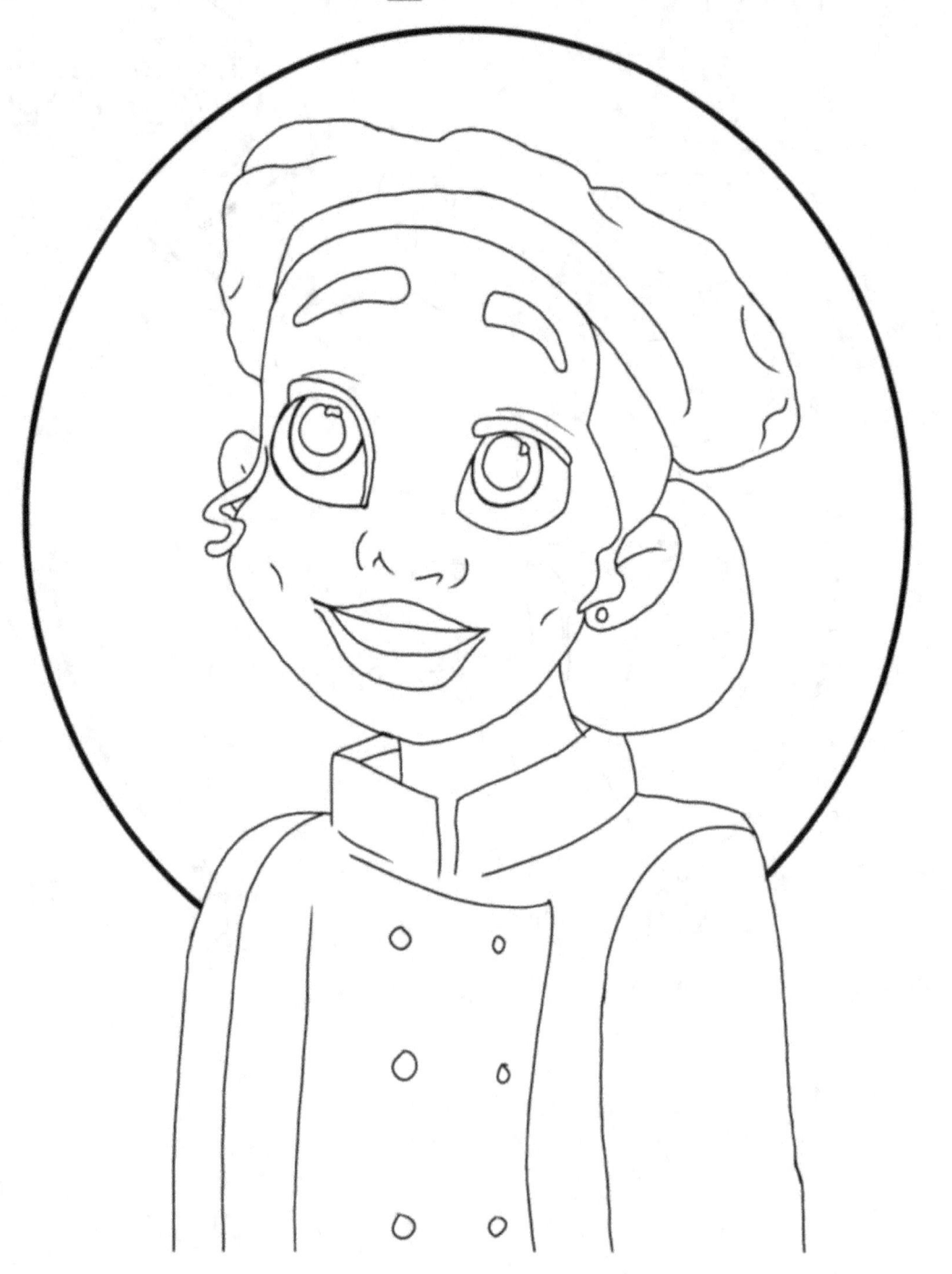

We are black love.

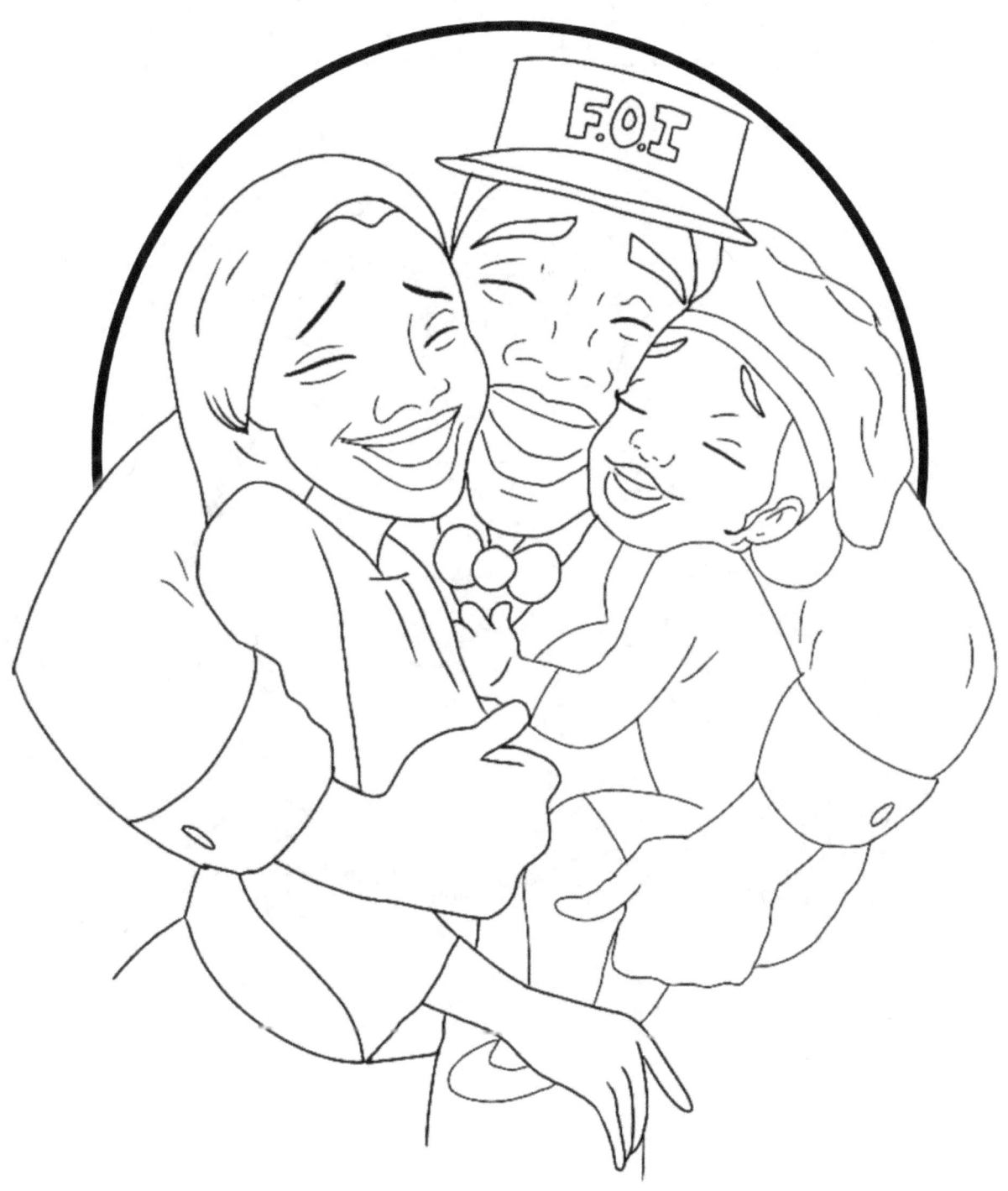

We are soldiers.

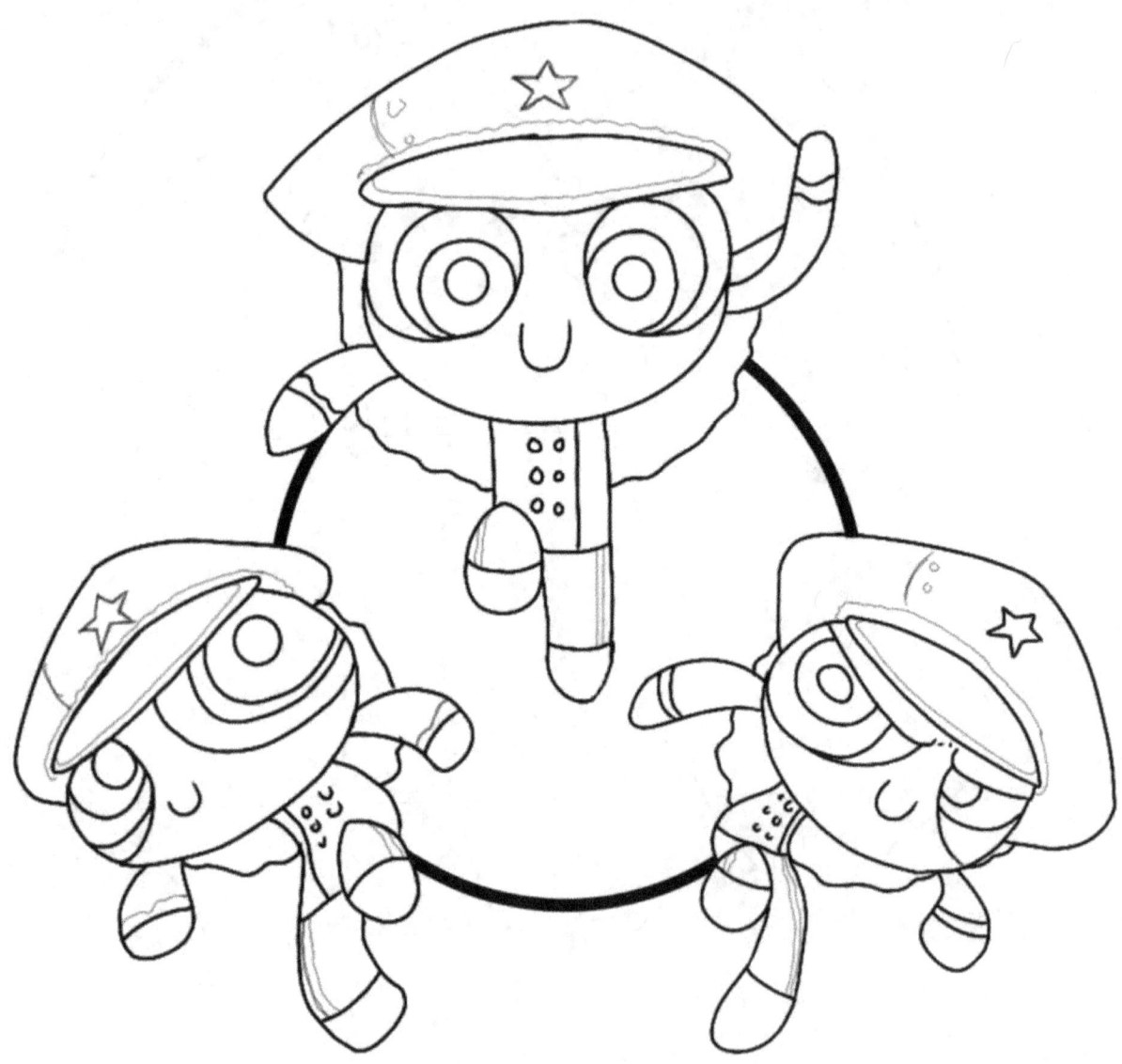

I am a defender.

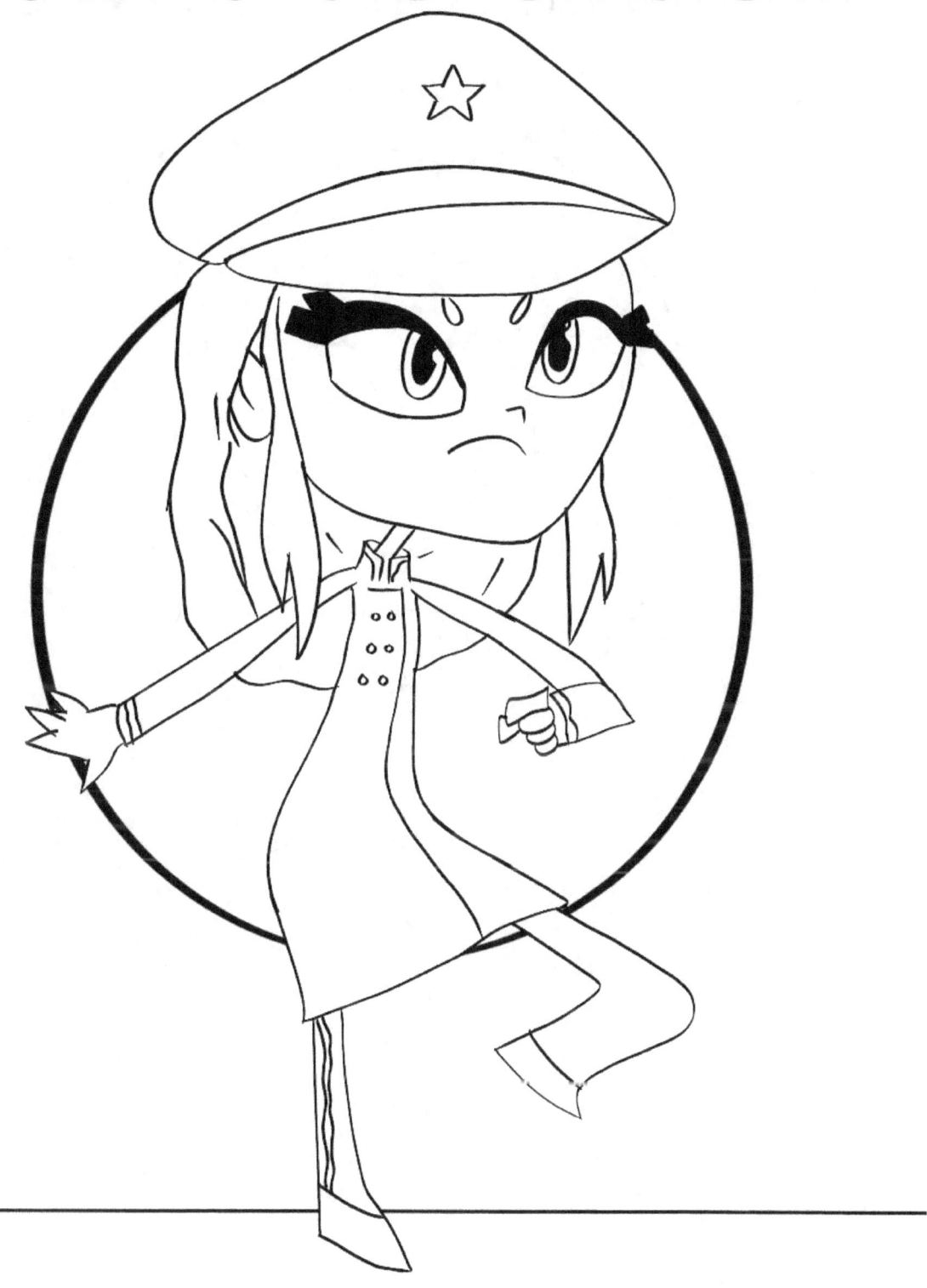

I am blessed.

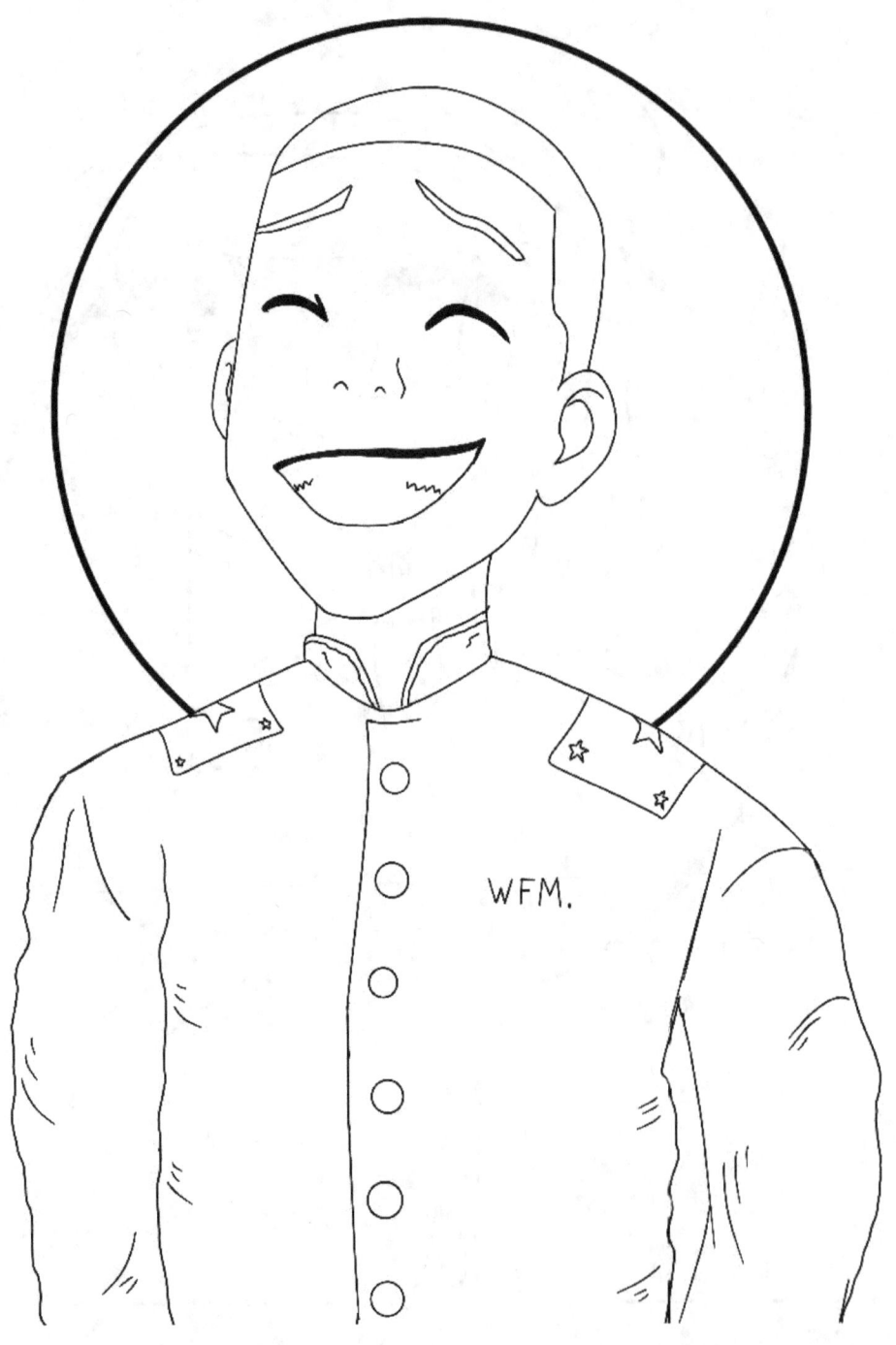

I am powerful.

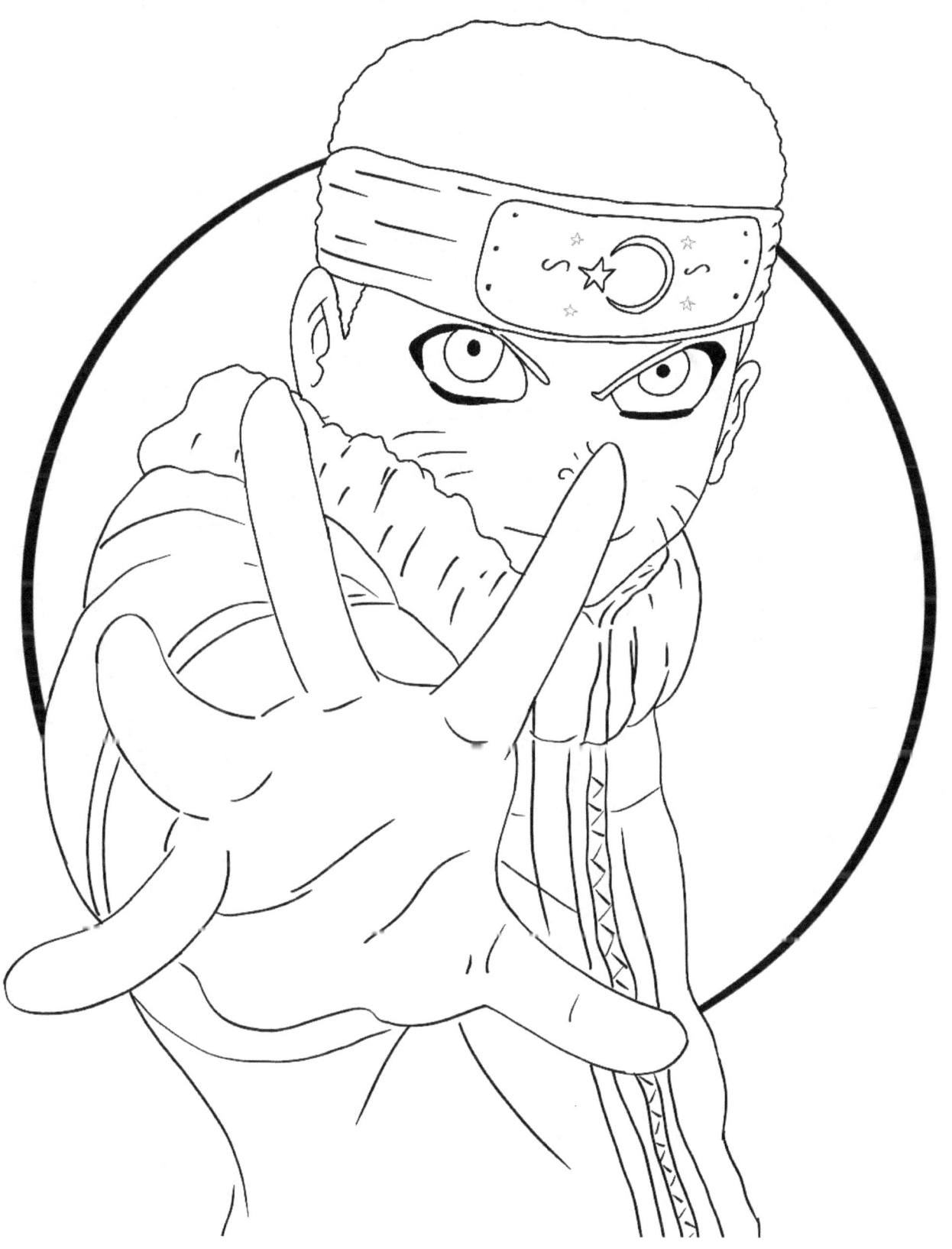

I am strong willed.

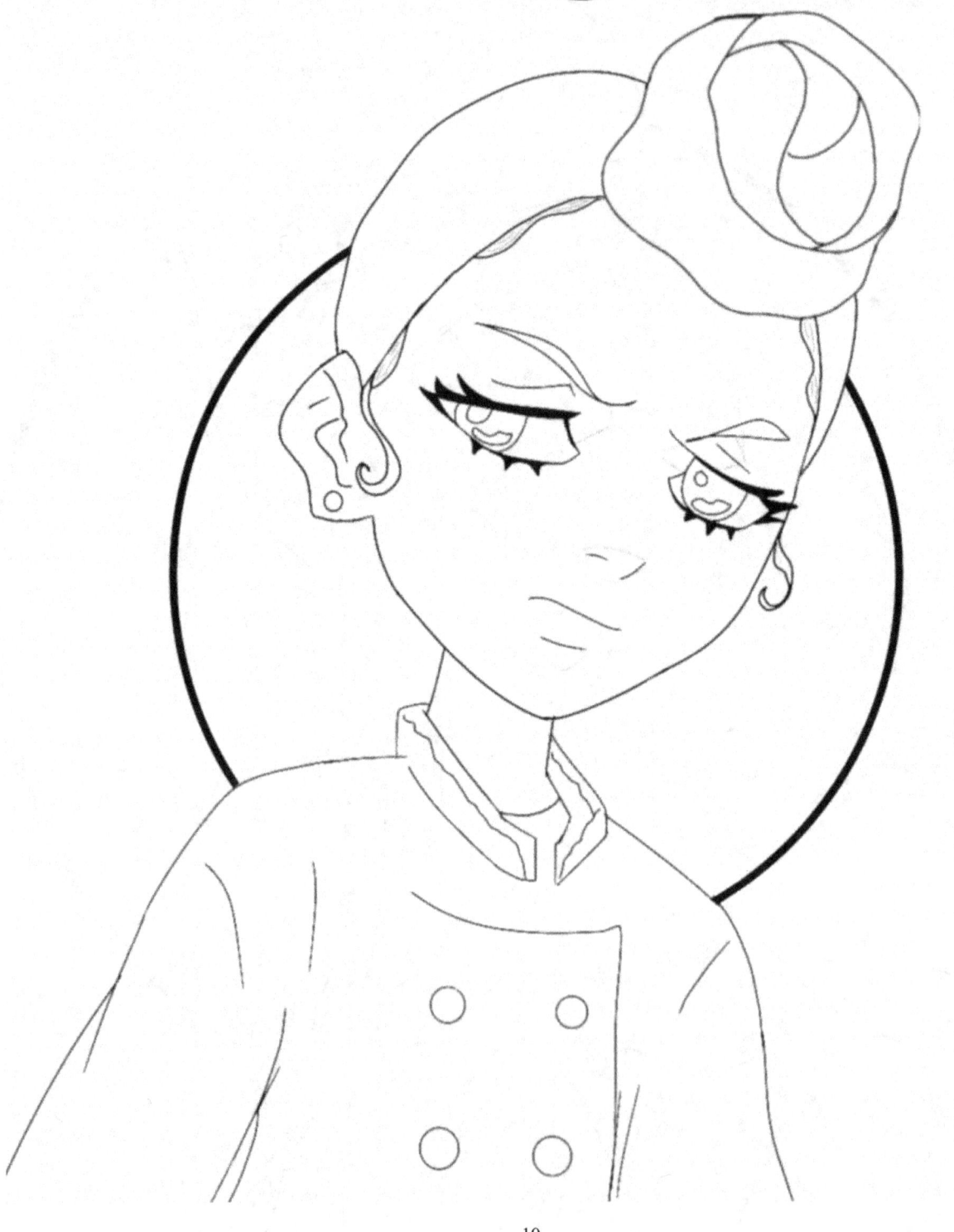

I am a young black man.

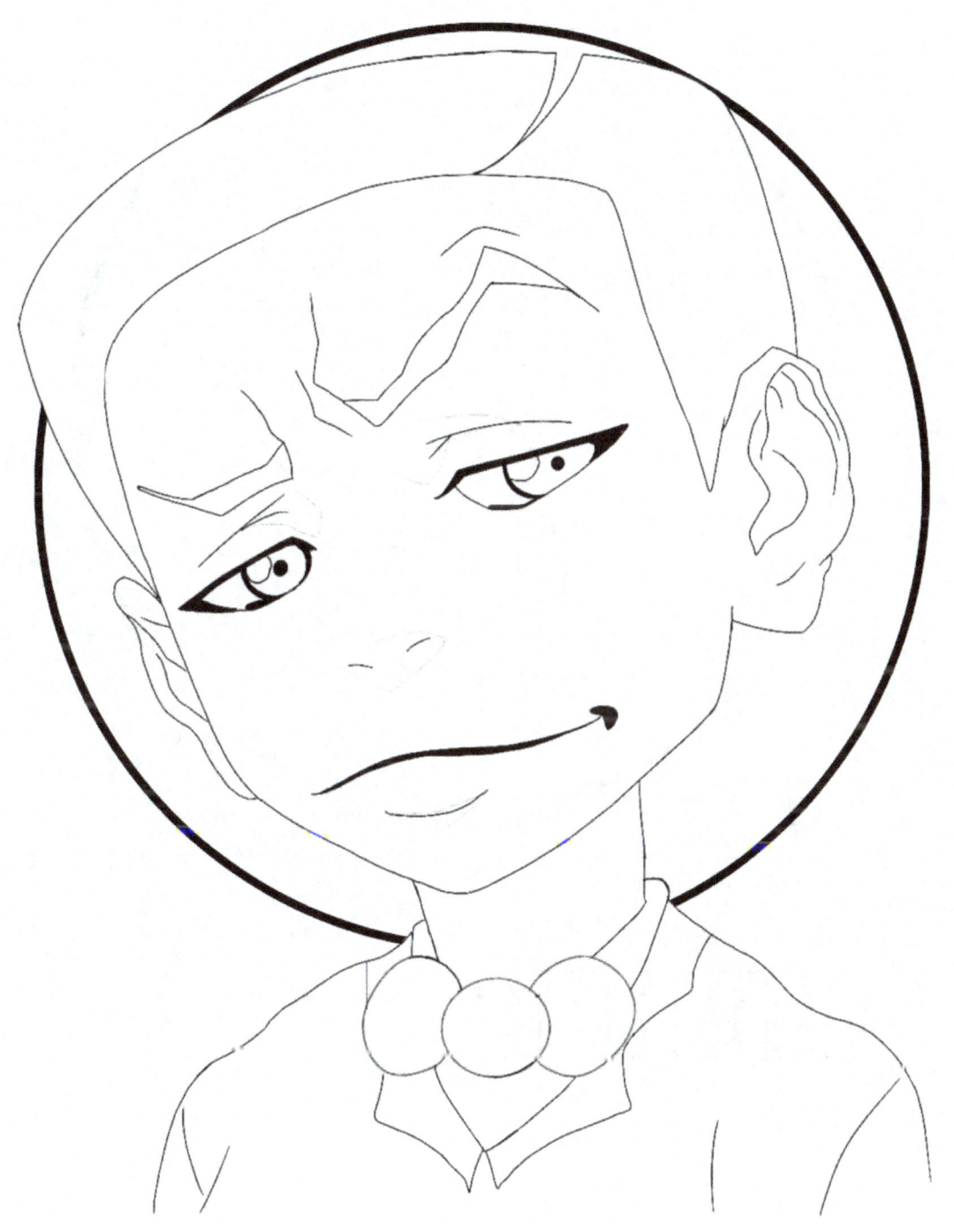

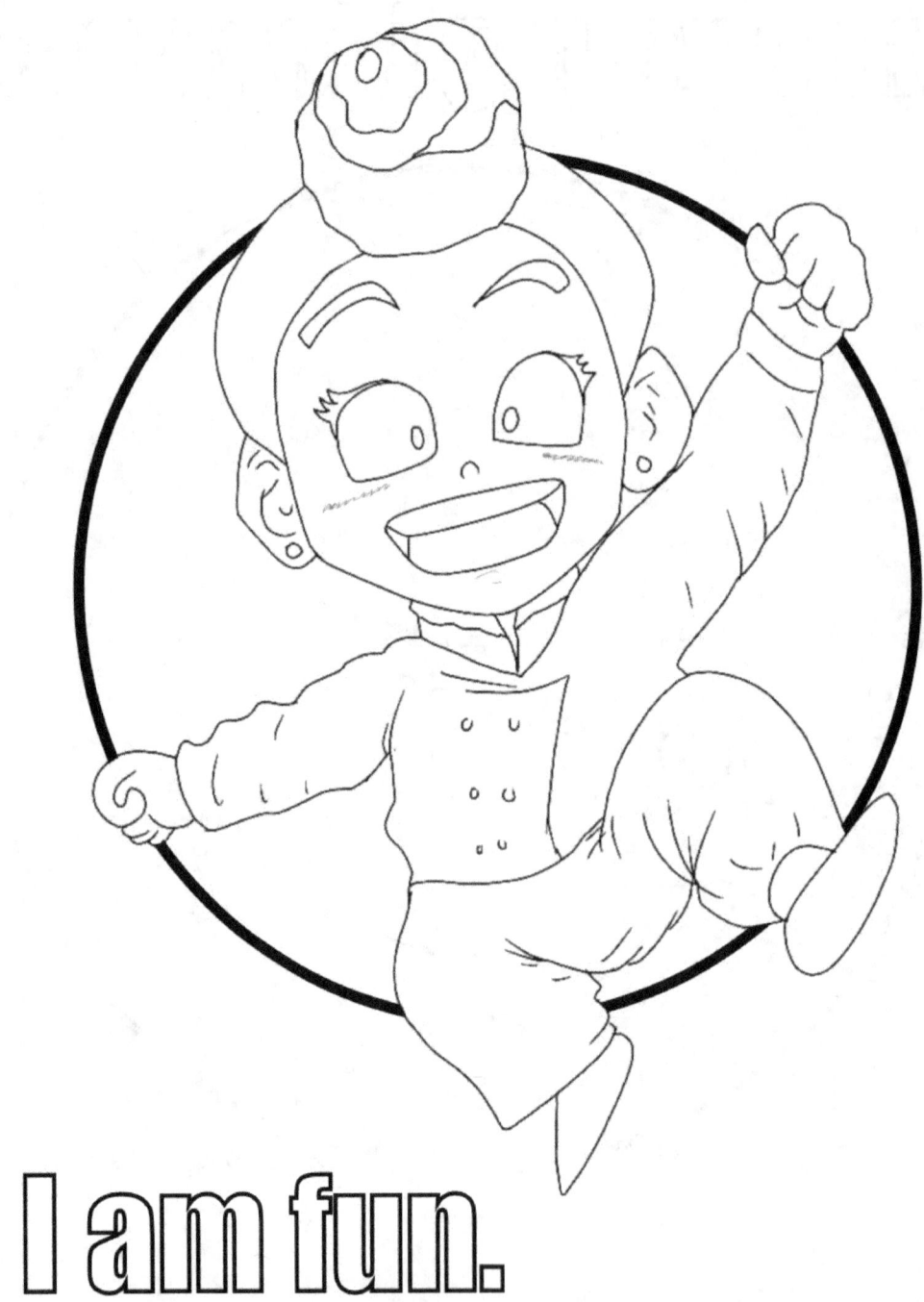

I am fun.

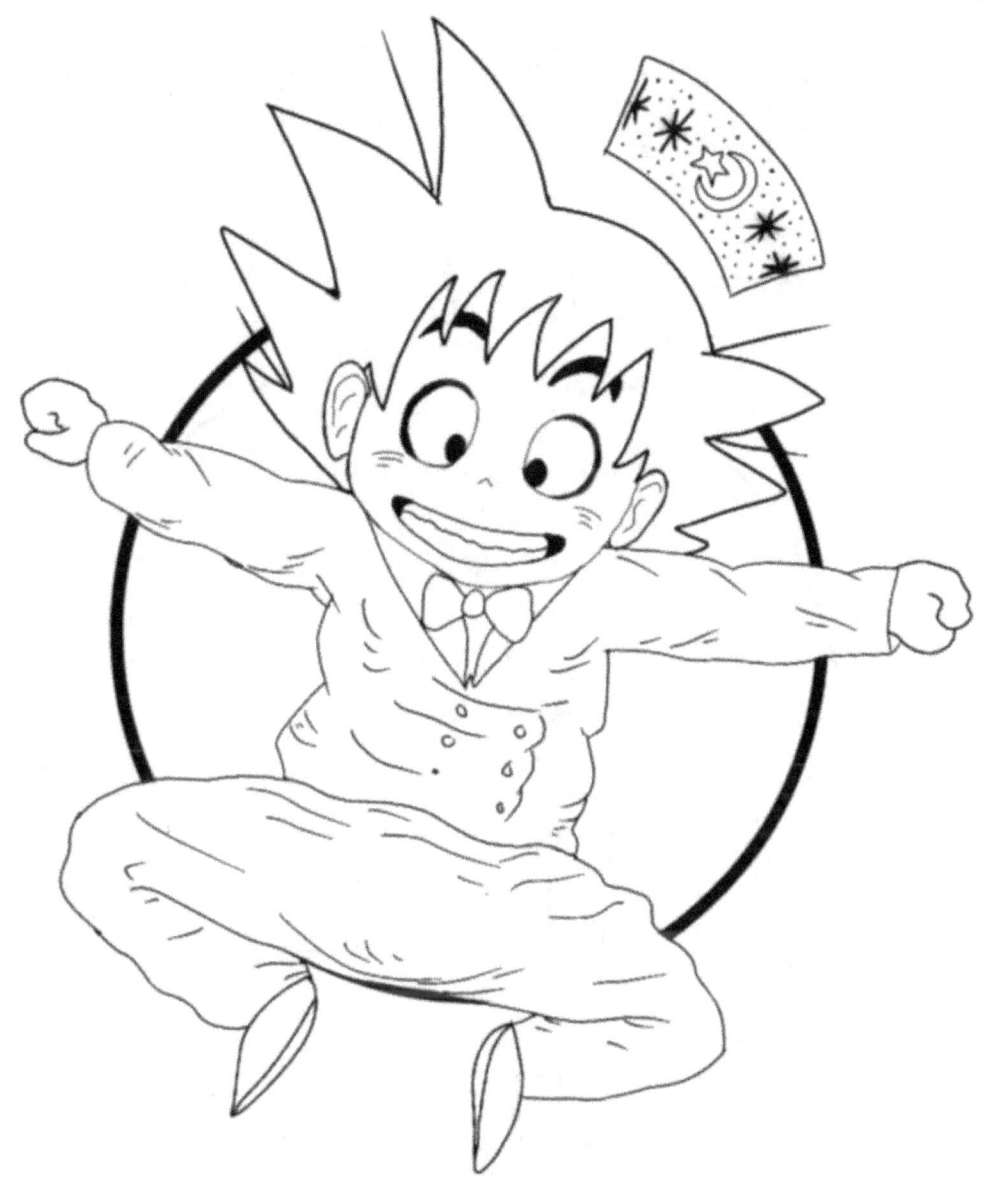

I am happiness.

I am determined.

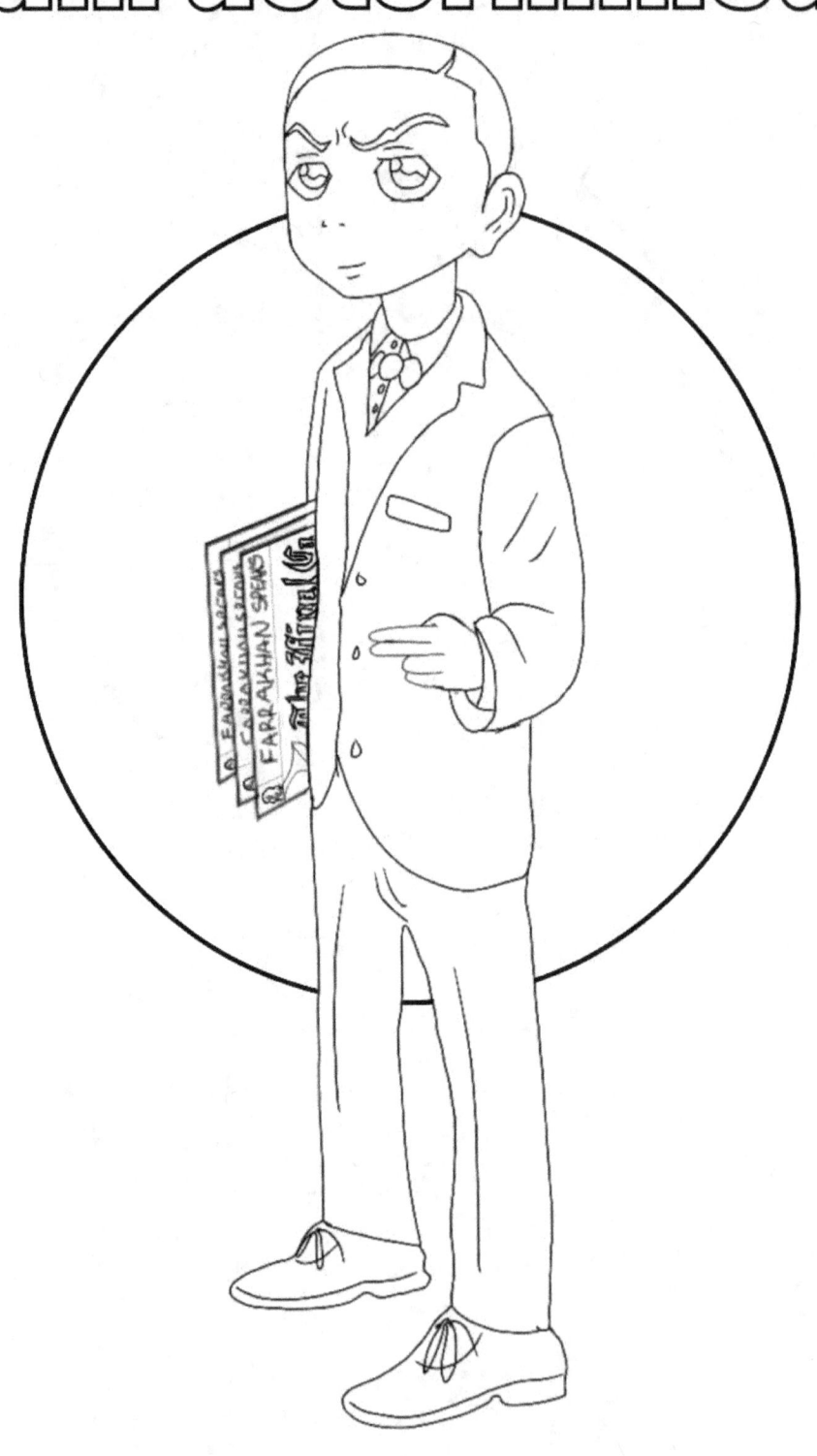

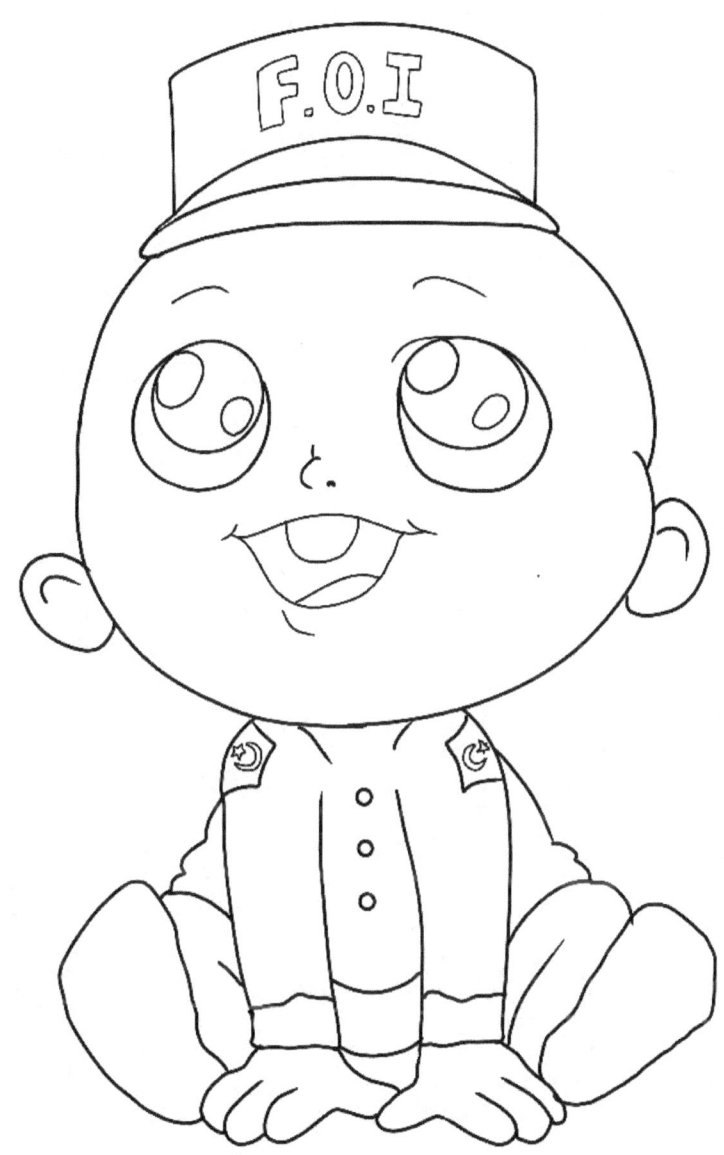

I am a baby god.

I am important.

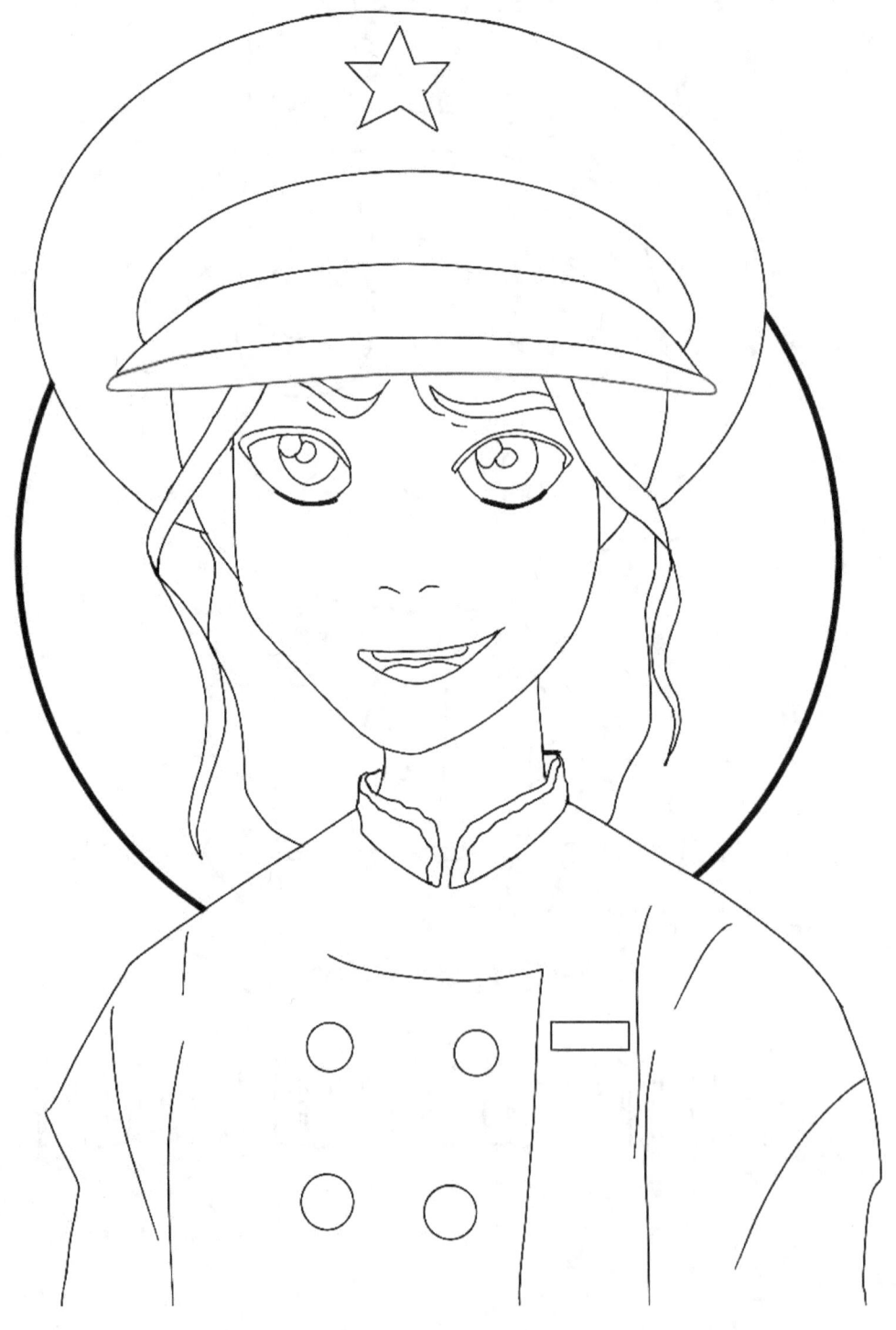

I am a Vanguard.

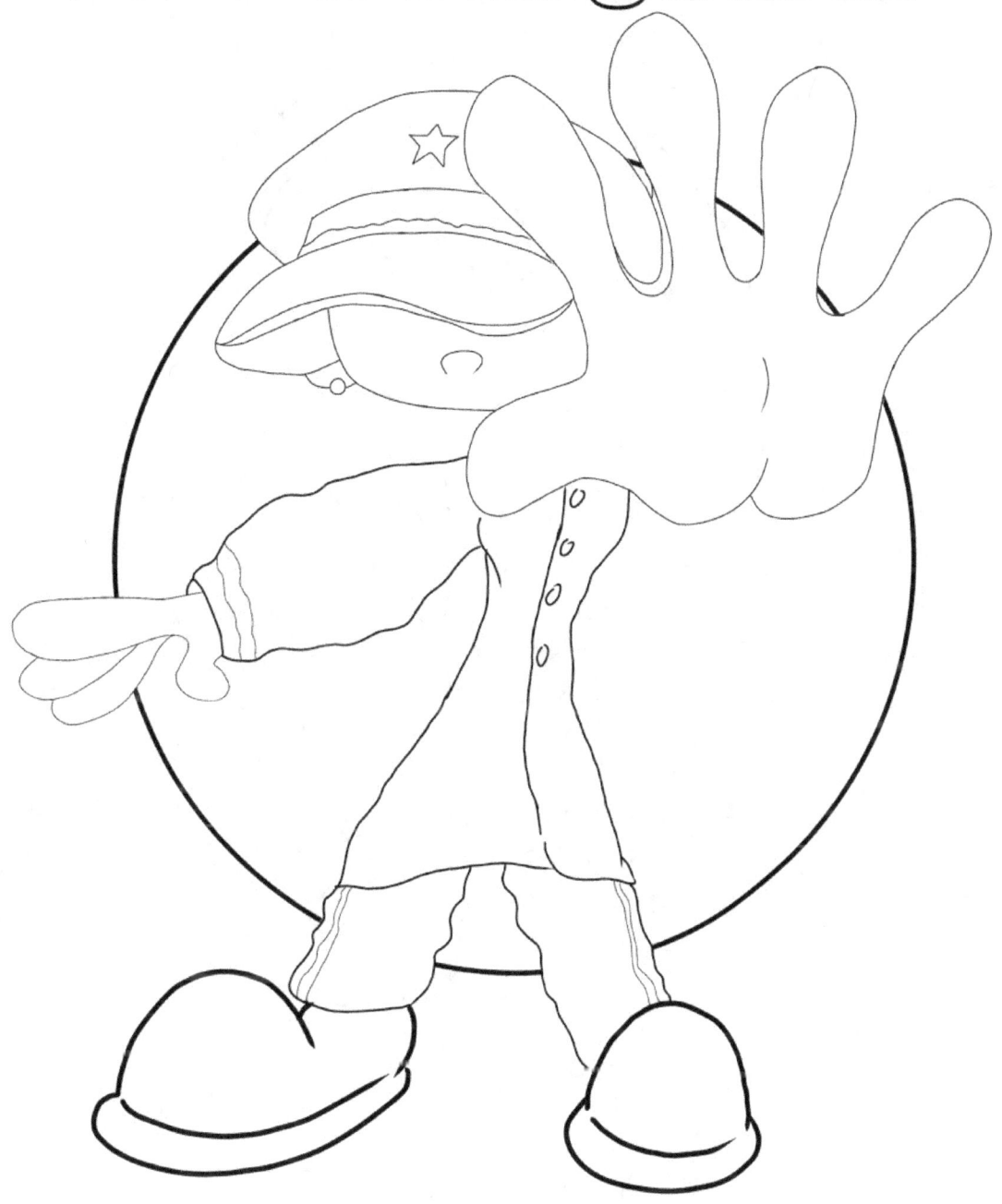

I am kind.

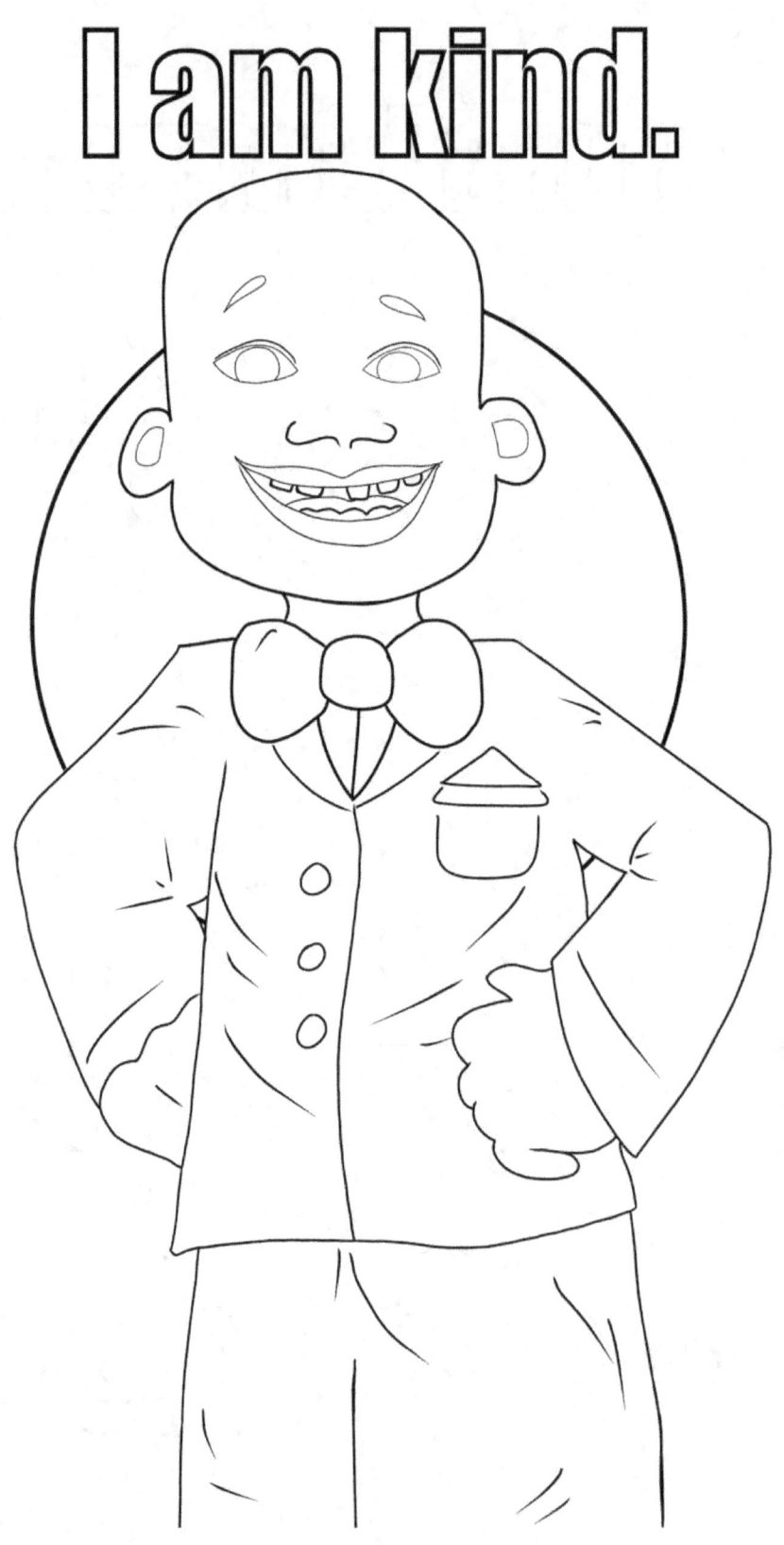

I am peace.

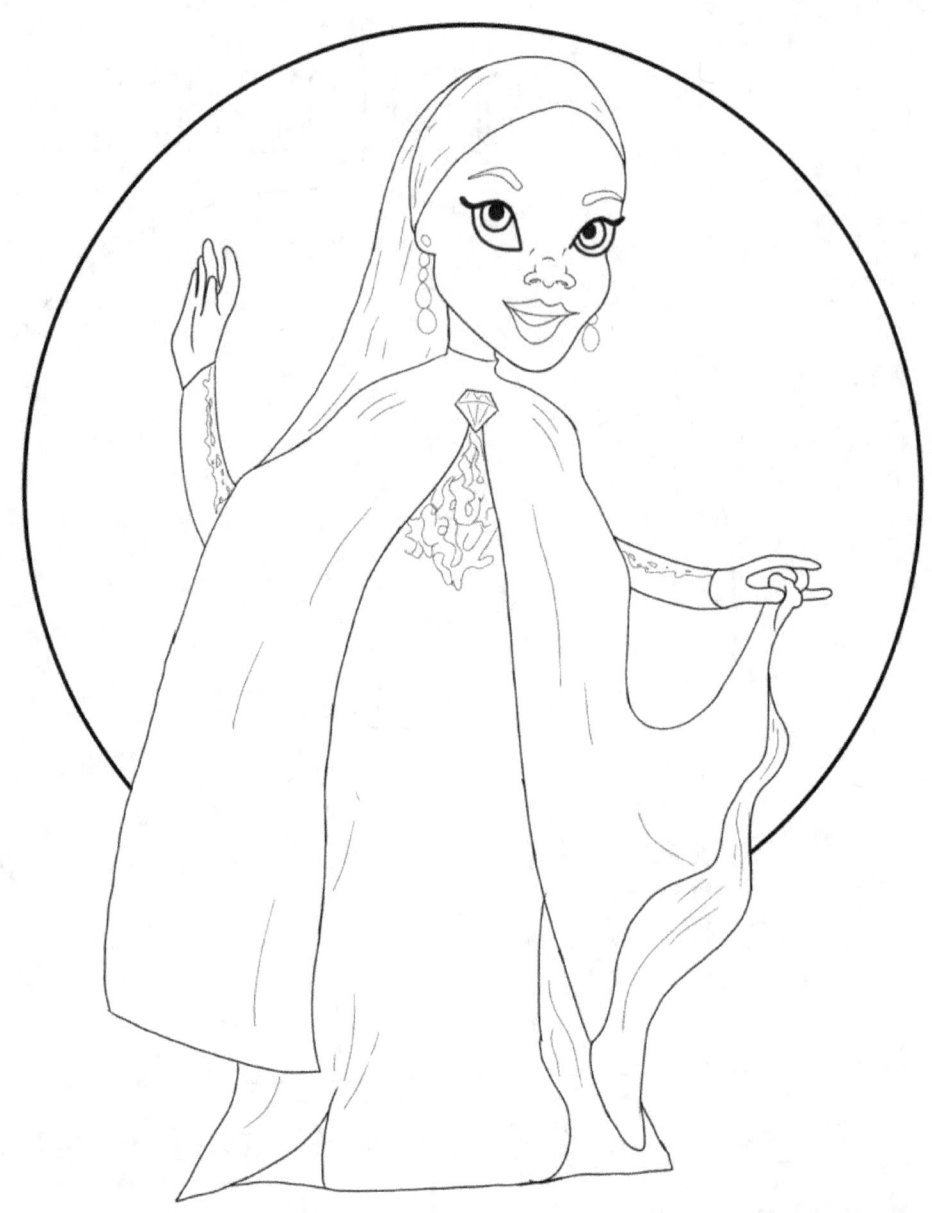

I am royalty.

I am strong.

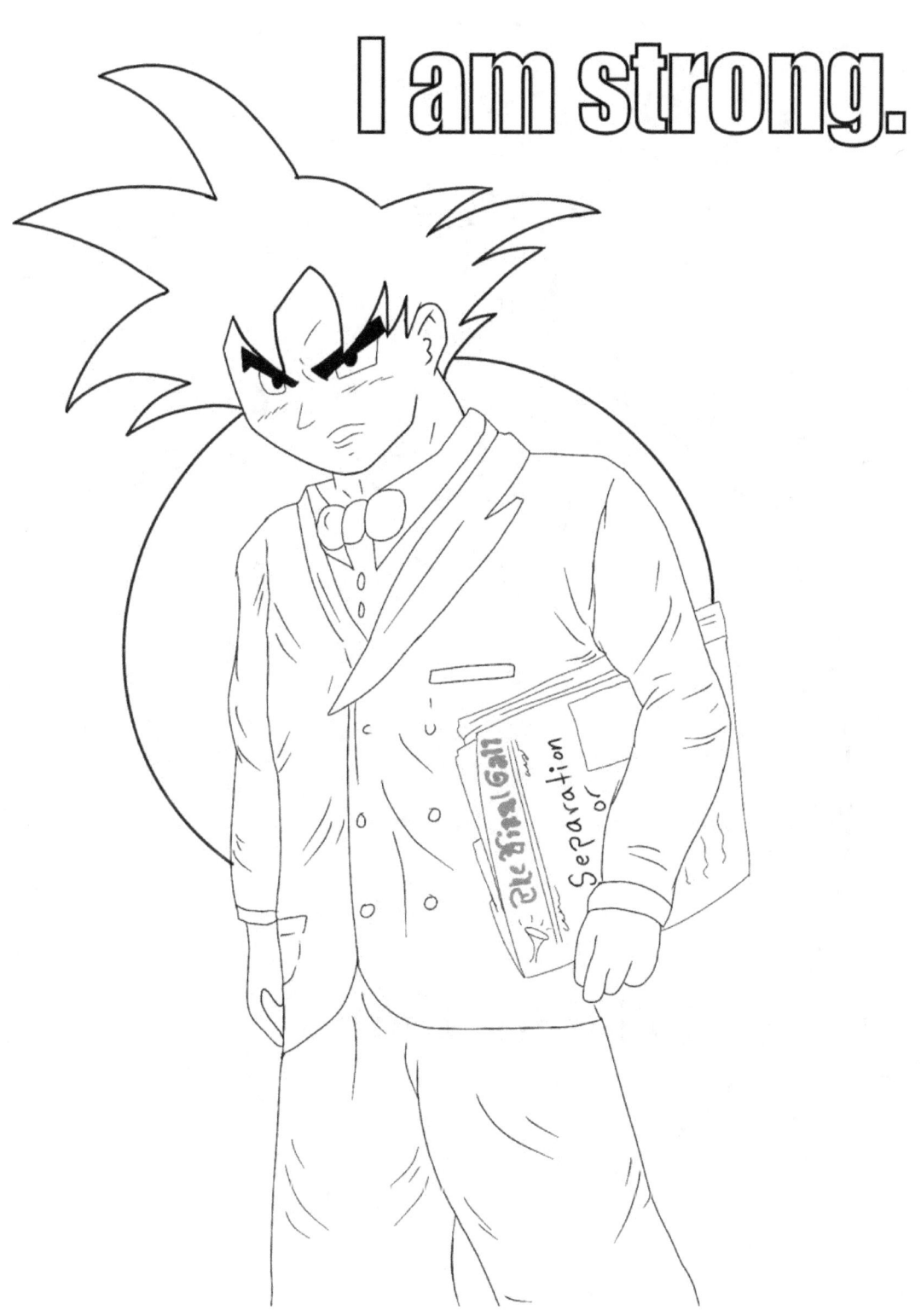

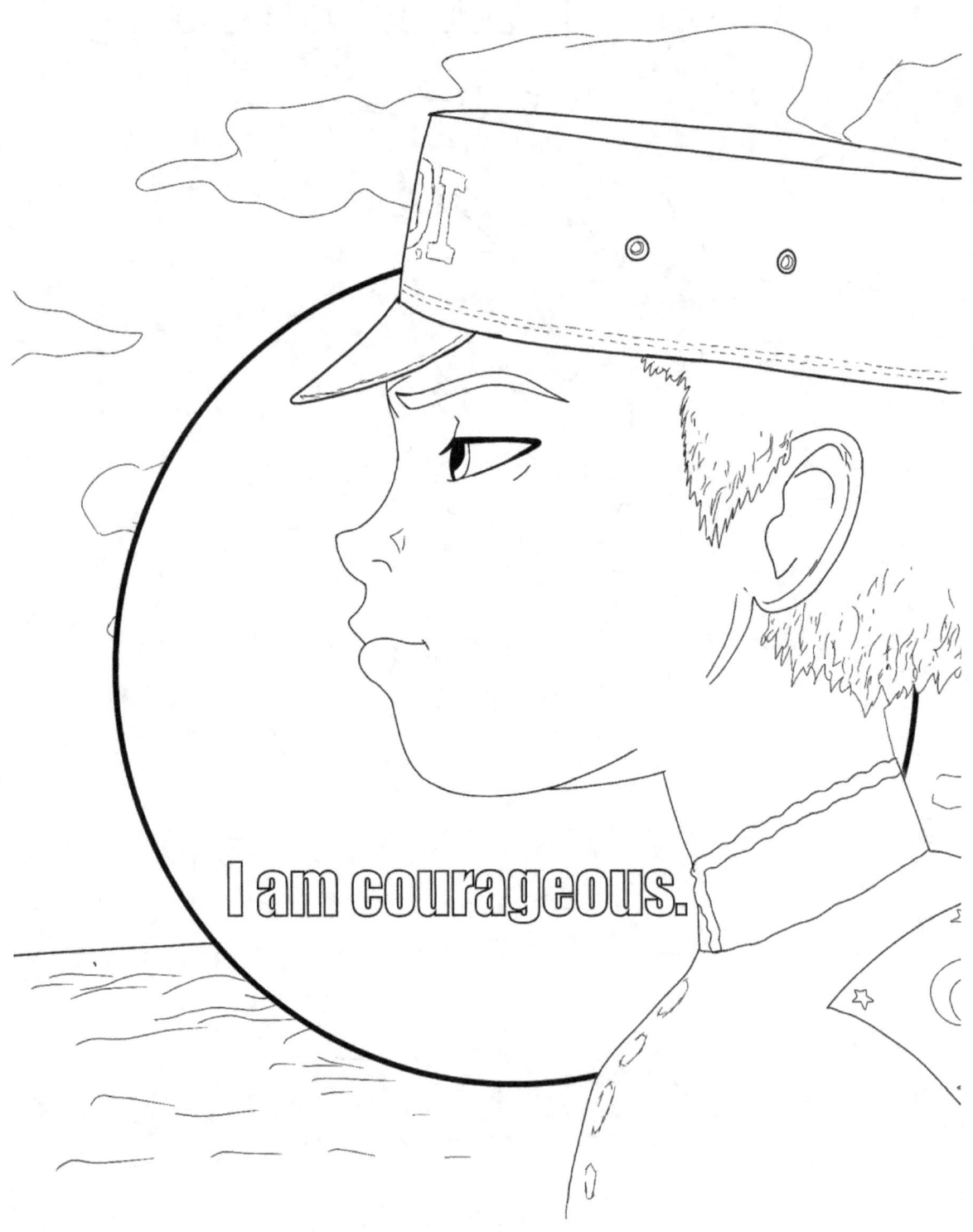

I am Farrakhan.

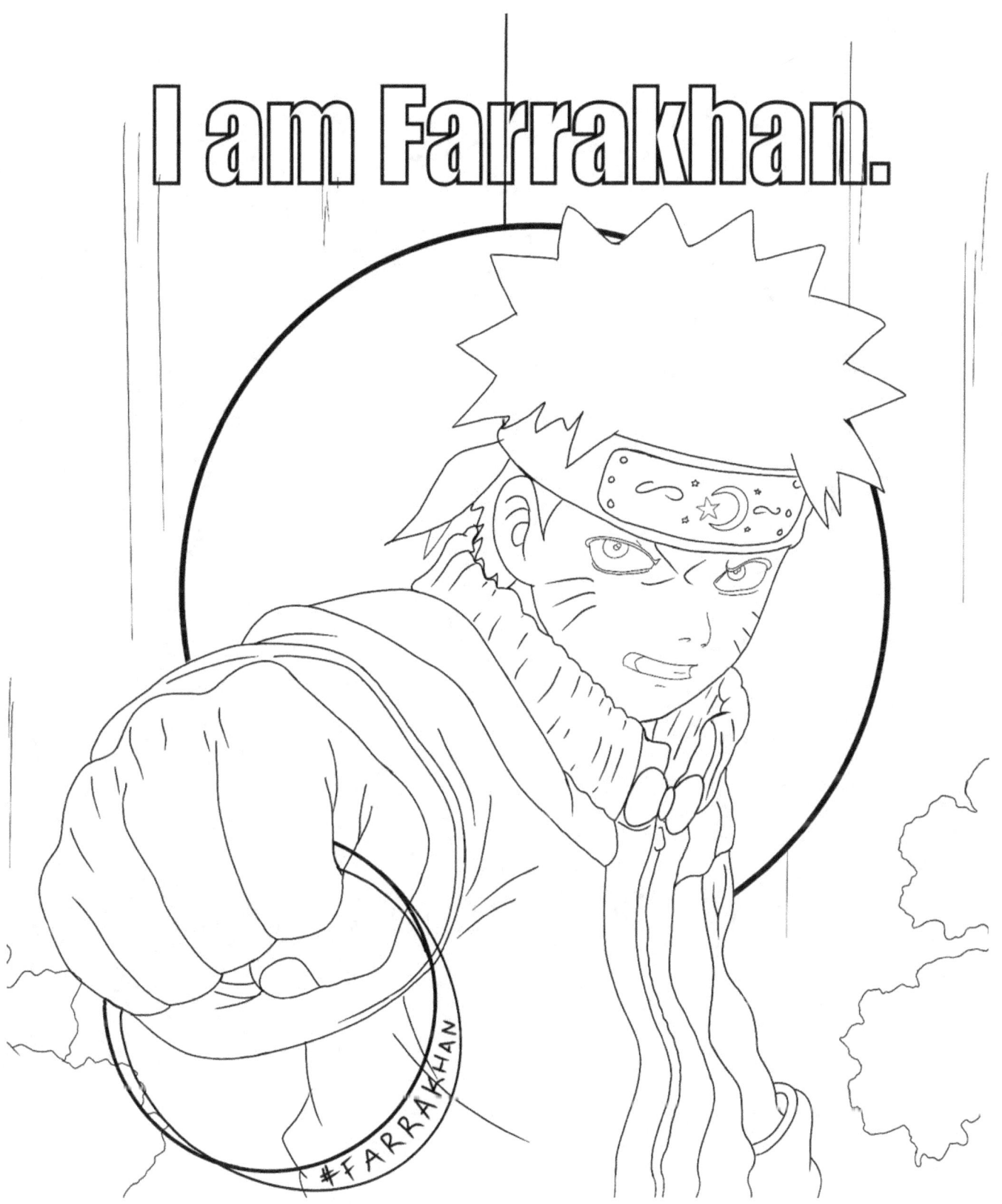

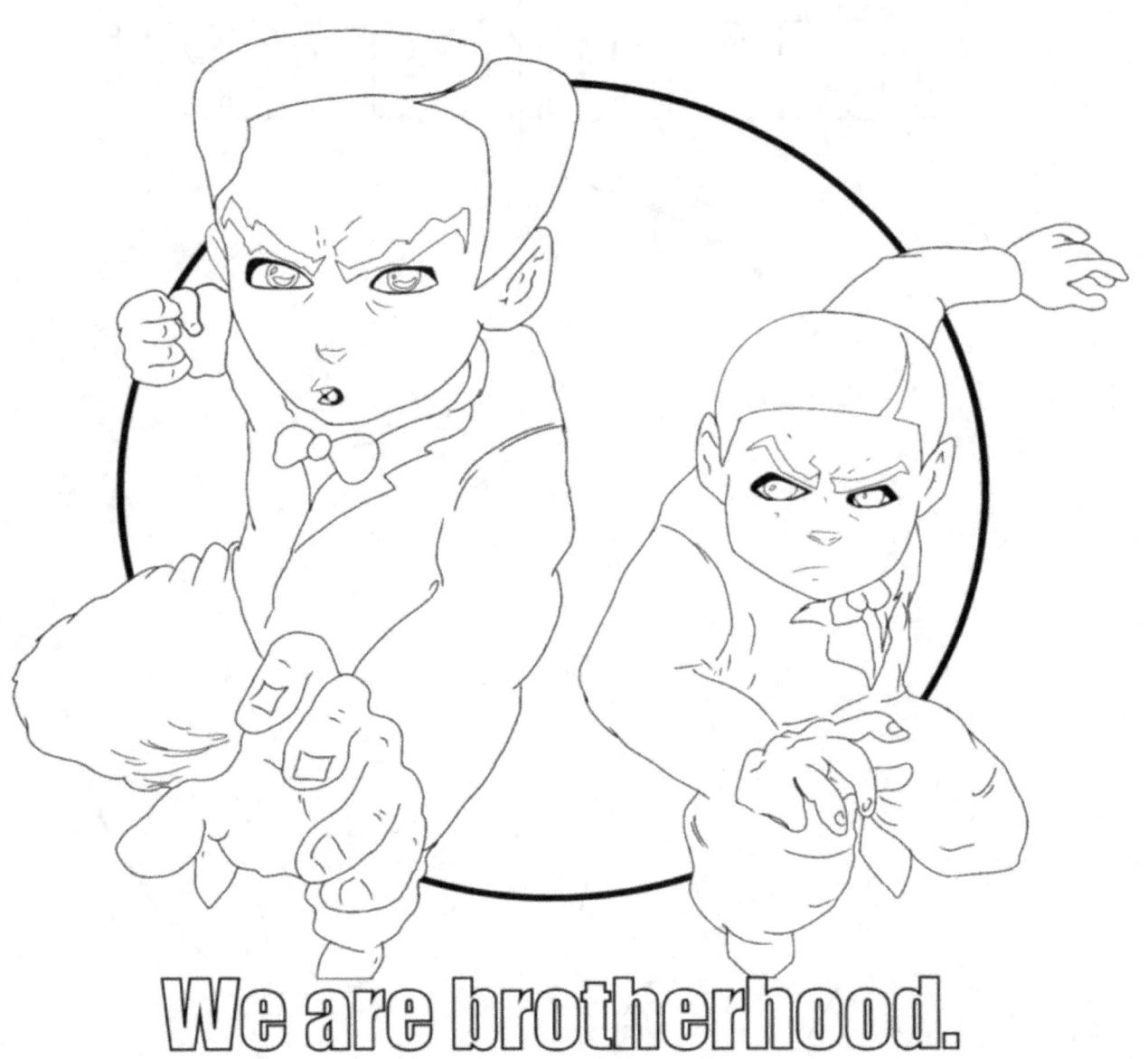

We are brotherhood.